GCSE Music
Listening Tests

AQA

Teacher's Guide

Andrew S. Coxon and Philip Taylor

RHINEGOLD
EDUCATION

www.rhinegoldeducation.co.uk

TEACHER'S GUIDE

This Teacher's Guide is designed to support *GCSE Music Listening Tests* for the AQA specification. Here you will find suggested answers to all of the questions, along with information about the tracks used. A full track listing is given on page 21 of this guide.

Please note there is no CD to accompany this book. All of the tracks used for these tests are available to download from iTunes as one album or 'iMix'. To purchase and download the iMix, please go to the *AQA GCSE Listening Tests* (second edition) webpage at www.listeningtests.co.uk, where you will find a direct link to the iTunes store.

AQA GCSE Music Listening Tests (second edition) uses 38 different tracks. You must acquire all of the tracks to complete all of the questions, but you may of course be selective about which questions (and therefore which tracks) you use. Although the iTunes recordings are recommended as the questions have been written with them specifically in mind, you can instead use recordings from other sources, such as CDs or online music players. Alternative options to iTunes are suggested in the help document 'Rhinegold Education Listening Tests instructions', which is available to download as a PDF from the *AQA GCSE Music Listening Tests* (second edition) page at www. listeningtests.co.uk. The document also gives help on using iTunes to play the tracks for these tests.

Once you have downloaded the tracks from iTunes, we suggest you re-arrange the order of the tracks to match the order of the questions (the correct order is shown below). For ease of putting the tracks in the correct order, Rhinegold has created an iTunes playlist for these Listening Tests, which is available to download from www.listeningtests.co.uk.

ORDER OF TRACKS

A full track listing can be found on page 21 of this guide.

THE WESTERN CLASSICAL TRADITION

Question 1	Mozart: 1st movement, Piano Sonata No. 16 in C, K. 545	0:00–0:30
Question 2	Fauré: In paradisum, from *Requiem*	0:00–1:00
Question 3	Beethoven: 2nd movement, Symphony No. 7	0:00–0:41
Question 4	Bach: Prelude No. 1 in C major from *The Well-tempered Clavier*	0:00–0:39
Question 5	Mahler: 2nd movement, Symphony No. 1	0:00–0:50 (fade)
Question 6	Mendelssohn: 2nd movement, Octet in E♭	0:00–0:50
Question 7	Arnold: 3rd movement, English Dances Set 1	0:00–1:53
Question 8	Tchaikovsky: 4th movement, Symphony No. 6	2:33–4:21
Question 9	Haydn: 2nd movement, Thema, from Op.76 No. 3	complete track
Question 10	di Capua/Capurro: 'O sole mio'	0:00–1:19
Question 11	Wagner: 'Bridal Choir' from *Lohengrin*	0:00–0:27
Question 12	Mozart: 1st movement, Piano Sonata No. 11 in A, K. 331	0:00–0:24
Question 13	Bach: 2nd movement, Concerto for two violins in D minor	0:00–0:50

POPULAR MUSIC OF THE 20TH AND 21ST CENTURIES

Question 14	Greenfield, Black and Cornwell: 'Golden Brown'	0:00–1:11
Question 15	Berryman, Buckland, Champion and Martin: 'Clocks'	0:00–1:13
Question 16	Stewart and Goldman: 'Wall Street Shuffle'	0:00–0:49
Question 17	Rogers and Hammerstein: 'The farmer and the cowman', from *Oklahoma!*	0:00–1:04
Question 18	Lordan: 'Apache'	0:00–0:40
Question 19	John: Finale, from *Billy Elliot*	0:00–1:21
Question 20	Weiss, Peretti and Creatore: 'Can't help falling in love with you'	
	version by Elvis Presley	0:00–0:35
	version by UB40	0:00–0:58
Question 21	Harry and Stein: 'Heart of Glass'	0:00–0:34
Question 22	Boublil and Schoenberg: 'Castle on a Cloud'	0:00–1:08
Question 23	Williams: Main theme, from *Schindler's List*	0:00–1:35 (fade)
Question 24	Dylan: 'Blowin' in the wind'	
	version by Bob Dylan	0:00–0:55
	version by Stevie Wonder	0:00–1:22
Question 25	Andersson and Ulvaeus: 'Thank you for the music'	0:00–0:42

WORLD MUSIC

Question 26	Cono	0:00–0:58
Question 27	Shakira	0:00–0:32
Question 28	Caribbean Steel Drum Calypso	0:00–0:42 (fade)
Question 29	Romeo and Perry: 'War Ina Babylon'	0:00–0:39
Question 30	Raga Bhaityar, Sitar	0:00–0:46
Question 31	Trinidad Steel Pan Reggae	0:00–0:42
Question 32	Island in the Sun (See note on page 19)	0:00–0:41
Question 33	He Govinda He Gopala	0:00–0:38
Question 34	Panjabi Clap	0:00–0:50
Question 35	Dance of the Hunters	0:00–0:42
Question 36	Simon: 'Homeless'	0:00–1:07

ANSWERS

The answers given here are intended as a guide – they are not always the only possible responses. Alternative answers should always receive credit if they form an accurate and unambiguous response to the question.

THE WESTERN CLASSICAL TRADITION

QUESTION 1

a. (ii) *(1 mark)*

b. acceptable answers: $\frac{2}{4}, \frac{4}{4}, \frac{2}{2}$ *(maximum 1 mark)*

c. Allegro *(1 mark)*

d. major *(1 mark)*

e. melody with accompaniment/main tune with accompaniment *(1 mark)*

Total: 5 marks

QUESTION 2

a. (church/pipe) organ *(1 mark)*

b. disjunct *(1 mark)*

c. treble *(1 mark)*

d. three *(1 mark)*

e. $\frac{3}{4}$ *(1 mark)*

f. major *(1 mark)*

Total: 6 marks

QUESTION 3

a. minor *(1 mark)*

b. acceptable answers: $\frac{2}{4}, \frac{4}{4}$ *(maximum 1 mark)*

c. violas (accept cellos) *(1 mark)*

d. strings *(1 mark)*

e. (ii) *(1 mark)*

Total: 5 marks

QUESTION 4

a. broken chords *(1 mark)*

b. (root-position) major (triad) *(1 mark)*

c. $\frac{4}{4}$ *(1 mark)*

d. piano/pianoforte (not just keyboard) *(1 mark)*

e. (iv) *(1 mark)*

Total: 5 marks

QUESTION 5

a. perfect 4th *(1 mark)*

b. octave *(1 mark)*

c.

(1 mark for each correct note; maximum 5 marks)

Sub-total: 7 marks

Extension questions

d. woodwind *(1 mark)*

e. major *(1 mark)*

Sub-total: 2 marks

Total: 9 marks

a. minor *(1 mark)*

b. string octet *(1 mark)*

c. acceptable answers: $\frac{3}{4}$, $\frac{6}{8}$ *(1 mark)*

d. Andante/Lento/Moderato *(1 mark)*

e. *mf*/*mp* *(1 mark)*

f. antiphonal *(1 mark)*; homophonic *(1 mark)*; melody with accompaniment *(1 mark) (maximum 3 marks)*

Teacher advice: in the actual AQA examination, there may be as many as eight options when candidates have to choose three.

Total: 8 marks

a. harp *(1 mark)*

b. bassoon *(1 mark)*

c. tremolando *(1 mark)*

d. con arco *(1 mark)*

e. piccolo (accept flute) *(1 mark)*

f. woodwind *(1 mark)*

Total: 6 marks

1 mark for each correct point. Maximum 2 marks for each repeat.

Second repeat: louder/octave higher/more instruments/off-beat accompaniment

Third repeat: louder/octave higher/trombones and trumpets imitate one bar later/ bigger crescendo at the end/melody takes a different course at the end

Total: 4 marks

Teacher advice: mark schemes are not always 'watertight' – students may find other details which may be valid and haven't been included in the mark scheme. If you are sure that it is correct, then award a mark. The most important attribute of a good examiner is to be consistent, so make a note of any additions to the mark scheme and apply it to everyone's answers.

QUESTION 9

a. AABCC *(1 mark)*

b. C *(1 mark)*

c. C *(1 mark)*

d. C *(1 mark)*

Sub-total: 4 marks

Extension questions

e. B *(1 mark)*

f. Poco adagio *(1 mark)*

Sub-total: 2 marks

Total: 6 marks

QUESTION 10

a. imitation *(1 mark)*

b. mainly conjunct *(1)*, mainly diatonic *(1) (2 marks)*

c. contains portamento *(1)*, contains a sequence *(1) (2 marks)*

d. (ii) *(1 mark)*

Total: 6 marks

QUESTION 11

a. trumpet *(1 mark)*

b. fanfare *(1 mark)*

c. major *(1 mark)*

d. acceptable answers: $\frac{2}{4}, \frac{4}{4}, \frac{2}{2}$ *(maximum 1 mark)*

e. homophonic/harmonic/hymn-like/chordal *(maximum 1 mark)*

f. mixed-voice choir *(1 mark)*

Total: 6 marks

QUESTION 12

a. acceptable answers: $\frac{6}{8}, \frac{3}{8}, \frac{3}{4}$ *(maximum 1 mark)*

b. **i.** imperfect *(2)*; or Ic/tonic second inversion *(1)* then V/dominant *(1)* *(maximum 2 marks)*

    ii. perfect *(2)*; or V/dominant *(1)* then I/tonic *(1)* *(maximum 2 marks)*

c. dotted rhythm *(1 mark)*

Total: 6 marks

QUESTION 13

a. major *(1 mark)*

b. $\frac{12}{8}$ *(1 mark)*

c. **i.** uses the same melody (allow other expressions) *(1 mark)*

    ii. begins on a higher note (allow other expressions) *(1 mark)*

d. harpsichord *(1 mark)*

Total: 5 marks

POPULAR MUSIC OF THE 20TH AND 21ST CENTURIES

QUESTION 14

a. harpsichord *(1 mark)*

b. $\frac{4}{4}$ *(1 mark)*

c.

(1 mark for each correct note; maximum 3 marks)

d. melody with accompaniment *(1 mark)*

Total: 6 marks

QUESTION 15

a. riff/ostinato *(1 mark)*

b.

(1 mark per correct accent; maximum 3 marks)

c. three *(1 mark)*

d. Similarity: same melody line (allow other expressions) *(1 mark)*

Difference: lower in pitch (allow other expressions) *(1 mark)*

Total: 7 marks

QUESTION 16

a. 4 (1 mark)

b. quaver *(1 mark)*

c. extra voice added *(1 mark)*

d. repeated *(1)*/octave leaps *(1)*/descending *(1)*/glissando *(1) (maximum 2 marks)*

e. **i.** falsetto

    ii. bass *(2 marks)*

Total: 7 marks

QUESTION 17

a. clarinet *(1 mark)*

b. acceptable answers: $\frac{2}{4}, \frac{4}{4}, \frac{3}{2}$ *(maximum 1 mark)*

c. major *(1 mark)*

d. piano/pianoforte *(1 mark)*

e. scalic/stepwise *(1)*, descending *(1) (maximum 2 marks)*

Sub-total: 6 marks

Extension questions

f. **i.** imperfect *(1 mark)*

    ii. perfect *(1 mark)*

g. F major/subdominant/IV *(1 mark)*

Sub-total: 3 marks

Total: 9 marks

QUESTION 18

a. **two** of: repeated/even/regular *(1)*, quavers/short notes/beats *(1)*, accent on every fourth note *(1) (maximum 2 marks)*

b. (electric) guitar (**not** acoustic) *(1 mark)*

c. pitch bend/using pick-up/using plectrum *(maximum 1 mark)*

d. AABA *(1 mark)*

e. four *(1 mark)*

Total: 6 marks

QUESTION 19

a.

(1 mark for each correct cross after the first; maximum 3 marks)

b. accel./accelerando *(1 mark)*

c. acceptable answers: $\frac{3}{4}$, $\frac{6}{8}$, $\frac{12}{8}$ *(maximum 1 mark)*

d. (drum) fill *(1 mark)*

e. big band *(1 mark)*

Total: 7 marks

N.B. each point must clearly refer to the correct version. Care must be taken to avoid rewarding the same comment more than once. Any valid points from:

	Version 1 (Elvis Presley)	Version 2 (UB40)
Rhythm	■ establishes triplet accompaniment rhythm straightaway ■ steady tempo/andante/moderato	■ one chord per beat to start ■ upbeat accompaniment rhythm when verse is repeated ■ strong accents ■ rhythmic changes (slight) to melody line during repeat of verse 1
Metre	■ 4 beats in a bar/ $\frac{4}{4}$ / $\frac{2}{4}$ / $\frac{2}{2}$ /feel of $\frac{12}{8}$ or $\frac{6}{8}$	■ 4 beats in a bar/ $\frac{4}{4}$ / $\frac{2}{4}$ / $\frac{2}{2}$
Texture	■ initially instrumental: broken chords over bass note ■ solo voice plus backing vocals added	■ initially solo voice over keyboard/synthesiser chords/melody with accompaniment
Melody	■ starts on keynote/tonic ■ opening leap *(1)* of perfect 5th *(1)*/ tonic to dominant *(1)*, returns to tonic *(1)* ■ stepwise movement to complete first phrase ■ second phrase starts lower/dominant ■ moves by step ■ ends on tonic	■ melody enters straightaway ■ starts the same as original version but, after initial leap of 5th, returns to tonic by step from 3rd/mediant ■ minor decoration of next phrase/upper mordent effect on 'help' ■ note of anticipation to final tonic (on 'you') ■ further slight variations to the rhythm of the melody in the repeat of verse 1
Timbre	■ bass guitar/double bass ■ piano ■ glockenspiel/celesta ■ solo voice *(1)* ■ male voice *(1)* ■ backing vocals	■ solo voice *(1)* ■ male voice *(1)* ■ initially plus keyboard/synthesiser *(1)* ■ drum kit added (to link to repeat of first verse) ■ keyboard/synthesiser now plays more rhythmic part ■ brass instruments/trumpets (to complete link to repeat of first verse)
Structure	■ instrumental introduction *(1)* ■ 2 bars of $\frac{4}{4}$ (or similar comment) *(1)*	■ first verse heard twice *(1)* with different style accompaniments *(1)*

Award a mark for any other valid point made.

Total: maximum 8 marks

QUESTION 21

a. acceptable answers: $\frac{4}{4}$, $\frac{2}{4}$ *(maximum 1 mark)*

b. 4 bars (only if the student's answer to question (a) was $\frac{4}{4}$) or 8 bars (only if the student's answer to question (a) was $\frac{2}{4}$) *(maximum 1 mark)*

c. percussion *(1 mark)*

d. glissando *(1 mark)*

e. echo *(1 mark)*

Total: 5 marks

QUESTION 22

a. pedal *(1 mark)*

b. (iv) *(1 mark)*

c. minor *(1 mark)*

d. interrupted *(2)*/V *(1)* – VI *(1)*/dominant *(1)* – submediant *(1)* *(maximum 2 marks)*

e. $A^1A^2B^1B^2$ *(1 mark)*

Total: 6 marks

QUESTION 23

a. oboe *(1 mark)*

b.

(1 mark for each correct note; maximum 3 marks)

c. interrupted *(2)* or V/dominant *(1)* – I/tonic *(1)* *(maximum 2 marks)*

d. perfect *(2)* or V/dominant *(1)* – I/tonic *(1)* *(maximum 2 marks)*

e. one octave higher *(1 mark)*

Total: 9 marks

QUESTION 24

Answers may include the following:

Timbre

- drumkit
- piano
- bass
- rhythm guitar
- saxophones added later
- second voice joins in later/singing in harmony

Rhythm and Metre

- tempo is slower
- swung quavers in drums
- triplet fills between lines
- crotchets and minims in bass
- rhythm guitar on offbeats
- vocal line more free in rhythm

Melody

- melody is decorated
- ornaments added
- extends some lines with extra notes at the end

Award a mark for any other valid point made.

Total: 8 marks

Teacher advice: If you feel there are further valid points which have been omitted, give credit where appropriate. Add to the mark scheme and be consistent in your assessment.

QUESTION 25

Rhythm

- ■ use of *rubato*/free rhythm/rhapsodic/*colla voce (1)* for first two lines *(1)*
- ■ more regular rhythm from line 3

Texture

- ■ single melody line with accompaniment
- ■ keyboard/piano/synthesiser plays linking phrases as soloist

Melody

- ■ opening rising arpeggio followed by short phrase moving mostly by step
- ■ improvisatory element to the piano part
- ■ 'I'm nothing special' all sung on same pitch *(1)* on tonic *(1)*
- ■ 'in fact, I'm a bit' sung to one pitch *(1)* a 4th lower *(1)* (extra mark for perfect 4th)
- ■ 'But I have a talent, a wonderful thing' moves around three notes *(1):* 4th, 5th, 6th of scale *(1)*
- ■ leap of 6th *(1)* (extra mark for major 6th) from 'cause' to 'everyone'
- ■ 'everyone listens when I' sung on one pitch *(1)* mediant/3rd (of scale) *(1)*
- ■ last two lines feature drop of 5th *(1)* (extra mark for perfect 5th)
- ■ extra mark for identifying modulation from tonic to subdominant
- ■ melody ends on dominant

Timbre

- ■ female voice
- ■ piano/keyboard/synthesiser
- ■ string sound introduced towards the end

Award a mark for any other valid point made.

Total: maximum 8 marks

WORLD MUSIC

QUESTION 26

a. crescendo *(1 mark)*

b. Any **two** of:

- Gan ko gui (allow shaker or double iron bell)
- Shekere (allow shaker)
- Djembe (allow hand drum or conga or bonga
- Djum djum (allow bass drum)
  (1 mark each; maximum 2 marks)

c. $A^1A^2A^1BB$ *(1 mark)*

d. tenor *(1 mark)*

Total: 5 marks

QUESTION 27

a. pentatonic *(1 mark)*

b. marimba (allow xylophone) *(1 mark)*

c. (ii) *(1 mark)*

d. **two** of:

- extra notes added (additional marks for detail)
- range of notes varies (additional marks for detail)
- rhythm of added notes varies (additional marks for detail)
  (maximum 2 marks)

e. two of:

- sustained/slow moving notes
- step-wise movement
- countermelody
- contrast of (melodic) style
  (maximum 2 marks)

Total: 7 marks

a. steel pans/drums *(1 mark)*

b. syncopation *(1 mark)*

c. $\frac{4}{4}$, but allow $\frac{2}{4}$ or $\frac{2}{2}$ *(1 mark)*

d. any **three** of: *(at least one point from each section; maximum 3 marks)*

Rhythm
- different rhythms heard alternatively at first *(1)* then simultaneously *(1)*
- rhythmic units *(1)*
- regular pulse/cross rhythms *(1)*

N.B. credit already given in question (b) for recognition of 'syncopation' so do not award a mark here

Texture
- individual timbres at first *(1)*
- variety of texture: imitative *(1)* polyphonic *(1)*
- layers of sound added progressively in first half/untuned percussion only in second half *(1)*

Total: 6 marks

a. homophonic/chordal *(1 mark)*

b. (i) *(1 mark)*

c. bass guitar *(1 mark)*

d. 2 and 4 *(1 mark for each correct answer; total 2 marks)*

e. quaver *(1 mark)*

Total: 6 marks

a. sitar *(1 mark)*

b. pitch bend *(1 mark)*

c. drone *(1 mark)*

d. three of:

- irregular/free pulse/*tempo rubato*
- changing sense of time signature/neither simple nor compound time sustained
- varied rhythms
- syncopation
- no pulse provided by the underlying drone – merely sustained notes rather than a rhythmic drone

Award a mark for any other valid point made.

(1 mark for each point; maximum 3 marks)

Total: 6 marks

QUESTION 31

a. minor *(1 mark)*

b. acceptable answers: $\frac{4}{4}$, $\frac{2}{4}$ *(maximum 1 mark)*

c. every two bars (only if the student's answer to question (b) is $\frac{4}{4}$) or every four bars (only if the student's answer to question (b) is $\frac{2}{4}$) *(maximum 1 mark)*

d. (ii) *(1 mark)*

Total: 4 marks

Please note that the version of 'Island in the Sun' used for Question 32 (from the album *Steel Drums of the Caribbean: Calypso Classics*, by the Jamaican Steel Band) is unfortunately no longer available on iTunes. It can be downloaded instead from amazon.co.uk or Spotify.

QUESTION 32

a. steel pans/drums *(1 mark)*

b. tremolo/sustained/chords/mostly in 3rds *(maximum 2 marks)*

c. 3 *(1 mark)*

d. bass (guitar) *(1 mark)*

e. acceptable answers: $\frac{2}{4}$, $\frac{2}{2}$, $\frac{4}{4}$ *(maximum 1 mark)*

Total: 6 marks

QUESTION 33

a. any **two** of:

- sitar/sarod/harp
- sarangi
- flute
- tabla
- tambourine
  (maximum 2 marks)

b. (in) octaves/heterophony *(1 mark)*

c. pitch bend *(1)*, repetition *(1)* *(maximum 2 marks)*

Total: 5 marks

QUESTION 34

a. (ii) *(1 mark)*

b. one note lower *(1 mark)*

c. reverb is added *(1 mark)*

d. third *(1 mark)*

e. (i) and (v) (*1 mark each; maximum 2 marks*)

Total: 6 marks

a. ostinato *(1)*, regular rhythms *(1) (2 marks)*

b. call-and-response *(1 mark)*

c. any **three** of:

- quite a wide range *(1)*
- usually opens with a leap *(1)* upwards *(1)*
- some use of pitch bend/*portamento (1)*
- first part of phrase stays fairly high *(1)*
- second part of phrase swoops down *(1)* then back up *(1)*
- all four phrases are basically the same *(1)*

Award a mark for any other valid point made.

(1 mark for each point; maximum 3 marks)

Total: 6 marks

a. call-and-response *(1 mark)*

b. major *(1 mark)*

c. diatonic *(1)*, homophonic *(1) (total 2 marks)*

Total: 4 marks

The track listings below are laid out with the following information:

Name of track
Artist, *Album*

THE WESTERN CLASSICAL TRADITION

Question 1
Mozart: 1st movement, Piano Sonata No. 16 in C, K. 545
Mitsuko Uchida, *Mozart: Piano Sonatas Nos. 8, 11 "Alla Turca", 16 & 18*

Question 2
Fauré: In paradisum, from Requiem
King's College Choir Cambridge & New Philharmonia Orchestra, *The Most Relaxing Classical Music in the World...Ever!*

Question 3
Beethoven: 2nd movement, Symphony No. 7
Daniel Barenboim, *Beethoven: Symphonies 1-9*

Question 4
Bach: Prelude No. 1 in C major from The Well-tempered Clavier
Jenö Jandó, *The Very Best of Bach*

Question 5
Mahler: 2nd movement, Symphony No. 1
Royal Liverpool Philharmonic Orchestra, Gerard Schwarz, *Schwarz Conducts Mahler 1*

Question 6
Mendelssohn: 2nd movement, Octet in E flat
Primavera Chamber Ensemble, *Mendelssohn: Octet & Quintet No. 2*

Question 7
Arnold: 3rd movement, English Dances Set 1
London Philharmonic Orchestra & Sir Malcolm Arnold, *Arnold: English, Irish, Scottish and Cornish Dances, Solitaire*

Question 8
Tchaikovsky: 4th movement, Symphony No. 6
Mariss Jansons & Oslo Philharmonic Orchestra, *Tchaikovsky: Symphony No. 6, "Pathétique"*

Question 9
Haydn: 2nd movement, Thema, from Op.76 No. 3
Alban Berg Quartet, *Alban Berg Quartett – Hommage*

Question 10
di Capua/Capurro: 'O sole mio'
Luciano Pavarotti, *Luciano Pavarotti: Classical Highlights, The Most Famous Hits, Vol.3*

Question 11
Wagner: 'Bridal Choir' from Lohengrin
Latvian State Symphony Orchestra Vilumanis & Riga Radio Choir, *MARCHES GREATEST HITS Featuring Pomp & Circumstance March No. 1*

Question 12
Mozart: 1st movement, Piano Sonata No. 11 in A, K. 331
Michael Droste, *Mozart and Beethoven for Pets*

Question 13
Bach: 2nd movement, Concerto for two violins in D minor
English Chamber Orchestra, Isaac Stern, Itzhak Perlman, London Symphony Orchestra & Zubin Mehta, *Bach: "Double" Concerto for Two Violins, Violin Concertos Nos. 1 & 2 (Expanded Edition)*

POPULAR MUSIC OF THE 20TH AND 21ST CENTURIES

Question 14
Greenfield, Black and Cornwell: 'Golden Brown'
The Stranglers, *Greatest Hits 1977-1990*

Question 15
Berryman, Buckland, Champion and Martin: 'Clocks'
Coldplay, *Clocks - Single*

Question 16
Stewart and Goldman: 'Wall Street Shuffle'
10cc, *The Very Best of 10cc*

Question 17
Rogers and Hammerstein: 'The farmer and the cowman', from Oklahoma!
Various Artists, *Oklahoma!*

Question 18
Lordan: 'Apache'
The Shadows, *The Shadows: Collection*

Question 19
John: Finale, from Billy Elliot
Original Cast of Billy Elliot, *Billy Elliot, The Musical – The Original Cast Recording*

Question 20
Weiss, Peretti and Creatore: 'Can't help falling in love with you'
Elvis Presley, *Elvis 30 #1 Hits*
UB40, *Love Songs*

Question 21
Harry and Stein: 'Heart of Glass'
Blondie, *The Best of Blondie*

Question 22
Boublil and Schönberg: 'Castle on a Cloud'
Les Misérables – 10th Anniversary Concert, *Les Misérables – 10th Anniversary Concert*

Question 23
Williams: Main theme, from Schindler's List
Royal Philharmonic Orchestra, *Movie Legends: The Music of John Williams*

Question 24
Dylan: 'Blowin' in the wind'
Bob Dylan, *Biograph*
Stevie Wonder, *Essential Stevie Wonder*

Question 25
Andersson and Ulvaeus: 'Thank you for the music'
The Abba Tribute Band, *Mamma Mia! It's the Abba Tribute Band*

WORLD MUSIC

Question 26
Cono
Salif Keita, *Soro*

Question 27
Shakira
All Star African Drum Ensemble, *African and Middle Eastern Drums: Belly Dance and Soukous Music*

Question 28
Caribbean Steel Drum Calypso
Caribbean Party Music: Jamaican, Calypso, Steel Drums and Other Music of the Caribbean

Question 29
Romeo and Perry: 'War Ina Babylon'
Max Romeo, *Island 40th Anniversary, Vol. 5: Reggae Roots 1972-1995*

Question 30
Raga Bhaityar, Sitar
Ravi Shankar, *Glimpses of Great Masters: An Indian Classical Music Sampler*

Question 31
Trinidad Steel Pan Reggae
Caribbean Party Music: Jamaican, Calypso, Steel Drums and Other Music of the Caribbean

Question 32
Island in the Sun
Jamaican Steel Band, *Steel Drums of the Caribbean, Vol. 2 – Calypso Classics*

Question 33
He Govinda He Gopala
Treasures of Indian Classical Music

Question 34
Panjabi Clap
Sukshinder Shinda, *Balle*

Question 35
Dance of the Hunters
Tribal Music on Location, African Tribal Music and Dances

Question 36
Simon: 'Homeless'
Paul Simon, *Ladysmith Black Mambazo: The Warner Brothers Collection*

First published 2010 in Great Britain by
Rhinegold Education
14-15 Berners Street
London W1T 3LJ
www.rhinegoldeducation.co.uk

© Rhinegold Education 2010
a division of Music Sales Ltd

You should always check the current requirements of the examination, since these may change.
Copies of the AQA specification may be obtained from
Publications Department, AQA, Devas Street, Manchester M15 6EX
Telephone 0161 953 1180 Fax 0161 273 7572. See also the AQA website at www.aqa.org.uk

AQA GCSE Music Listening Tests: Teacher's Guide
Order No. RHG164
ISBN 978-1-907447-00-6
Printed in the EU.

COPYRIGHT